LOOK AT THE SPARROWS

A 21-Day Devotional on
Financial Fear and Anxiety

FAITH FI

ISBN (Softcover Trade Edition)
979-8-9894556-1-4

Writing
Taylor Standridge, Chad Clark, Carolyn Calupca

Design
John-Mark Warkentin, Matthew Anderson

Logistics
Kevin Light

A special thanks to our team of reviewers for sharing their wisdom and knowledge with us as we worked together to create this devotional.

Printed in the USA

24 25 26 - 10 9 8 7 6 5 4 3 2 1

1st Printing

Welcome

The FaithFi team is delighted to present *Look at the Sparrows*, a devotional designed to help you explore God's Word on money and anxiety.

We wrote this devotional because we recognize that financial anxiety is a pervasive issue in our culture. Worry seems to surround us every day. From fear-inducing headlines to concerns about our jobs, bills, investments, and the future, anxious thoughts about our finances can consume us.

We've structured this devotional around the teachings found in Jesus' Sermon on the Mount, where he addresses the connection between our heart's treasure and anxiety (Matthew 6:19-34). Although this is not a verse-by-verse exposition of Matthew 6:19-34, we will explore some key themes within that passage.

Our prayer is that you will draw closer to God as you read this twenty-one–day devotional, seeing him as your ultimate treasure and experiencing the peace and fullness of his mercy and grace.

In Christ,
The FaithFi Team

Truth, Beauty, & Goodness

At the genesis of time, God's Word and breath initiated life in all of its variety, goodness, and esthetic beauty. At FaithFi, we believe God's true Word still takes center stage, and the use of beauty and creative storytelling is God's age-old method for bringing his good message to life for the contemporary church.

01

In this study, we make use of a black and white color system to leverage its strength and simplicity as well as its stark emotive characteristics. This helps to create a visual throughline to the emotions of fear and anxiety around money which can easily leave us feeling "colorless."

02

The addition of the color gold, represents hope in the midst of darkness. Gold catches rays of light and reflects them to the viewer, reminding us that God's promises and faithful character crowd out and overcome the darkness.

03

The image of the sparrow is one of God's incredibly kind assurances to the church. Carefree, dearly loved and provided for by God's eternal storehouse, the sparrow anchors each illustration in YHWH Jireh, the LORD who will provide.

04

Each illustration is meant to take the reader deeper into the meaning of a particular truth from scripture. As a parable conveys a spiritual truth through common visuals, the illustrations are meant to help you see with new eyes and stick with you as you journey through this study.

How To Use

This devotional can be used by individuals, couples, small groups, and churches.

Before you begin each day, ask God to reveal himself through his Word.

Use this study alongside your Bible. Each devotional references various scriptures; we encourage you to look them up while reading. If necessary, slow down and read the scripture and devotional multiple times. Avoid making this a daily checklist item you rush through.

The devotional is broken into seven sections based on teaching in Jesus' Sermon on the Mount, where he addresses "treasure" and "anxiety" in Matthew 6:19-34. Each section contains three daily devotionals. The first devotional of each section is taken from Matthew 6:19-34 while the other two devotionals build upon that section's theme.

At the end of each day, you will be asked to memorize that section's correlating passage from the Sermon on the Mount so that at the end of the devotional, you will have memorized Matthew 6:19-34. We encourage you to embed God's Word in your heart to draw your strength, hope, and peace from it throughout your days.

"For the word of God is living and active, sharper than any two-edged sword, piercing to the division of soul and of spirit, of joints and of marrow, and discerning the thoughts and intentions of the heart." (Hebrews 4:12)

To help you apply what the Lord is teaching you, each day is broken into the following sections:

Scripture Passage

Devotional

Pause

Pray

Ponder

Completing this devotional may take longer than 21 days, and that's perfectly fine. Take the time you need to fully experience the benefits of your time in God's Word.

Table of Contents

Introduction

Many people wrestle with financial anxiety, which can plague our lives and completely overcome our thoughts. Financial anxiety is not always dependent on how much money is in our bank account or the net worth on our balance sheet. Concerns about our jobs and income, bills, debt, investments, children, relationships, or broader economic and political uncertainty can leave us feeling anxious and even hopeless. Whether we're worried about not having enough or losing what we've accumulated, financial anxiety can impact anybody.

This study does not provide specific step-by-step guidance on overcoming any particular financial fear or anxiety; rather, it is intended to point you to a source of peace and joy that is not dependent on external circumstances.

The structure of this devotional is based on teachings found in Jesus' Sermon on the Mount that speak to both money and anxiety (Matthew 6:19-34). Although this is not a verse-by-verse exposition specifically on those teachings, we have drawn from those passages to guide us through scripture as we explore the topic of financial anxiety.

As you explore God's Word, we pray that you will find peace and strength in Christ to address your challenges and uncertainties. We encourage you to check out the Continue the Journey page at the end of this book to discover resources that may help with your financial situation.

Finally, we would be remiss to minimize the impact fear and anxiety can have on our overall well-being. Financial anxiety can be crippling. It can consume us and lead to many sleepless nights, depression, and potentially harmful thoughts. We encourage you to seek professional help if you suffer from these feelings.

We also invite you to bring your struggles to the great physician of our souls, Jesus. Cast your cares on him, trust him, and seek him with all your heart—because when you do, you will find rest and peace for your weary soul.

HEART'S *Treasure*

Day 01

For Where Your Treasure Is

— MATTHEW 6:19–21

Day 02

Finding Contentment

— PHILIPPIANS 4:11–13

Day 03

Incline My Heart

— PSALM 119:36–37

Day 01

For Where Your Treasure Is

— MATTHEW 6:19–21

19 Do not lay up for yourselves
treasures on earth, where moth
and rust destroy and where thieves
break in and steal, 20 but lay up for
yourselves treasures in heaven, where
neither moth nor rust destroys and
where thieves do not break in and
steal. 21 For where your treasure is,
there your heart will be also.

We fear losing that which we treasure most. The thought or possibility of financial loss can lead to crippling anxiety. Losing a job, income, home, possessions, savings, or investments are all very real possibilities. In fact, at some point, everything in this world will be lost, destroyed, or stolen. Yet, we continue to worry about the uncertain timing of certain losses.

When we treasure money and possessions, they take hold of our hearts as we seek protection, stability, and happiness from them. Placing our hope in money and its potential to solve our problems will lead us astray. While money can be a helpful tool, we should never put our hope in it.

Jesus tells us our treasure should not be found in the things of this world but in the kingdom of heaven. If money has a grip on our hearts, he tells us to sell our possessions and give to the needy because it is the Father's good pleasure to give us the kingdom (Luke 12:32). He wants us to take hold of that which is truly life, but to do so, we must let go of the things of this world that so often take our hearts captive. He must be our ultimate treasure.

Are there things you currently treasure more than God? Bring them to him. Ask him how he'd like you to deal with those things. If they are taking a place in your heart that rightly belongs to him, are you willing to do what is necessary to allow him to be preeminent in your life?

When we choose to trust God, we learn to hold things loosely. If he asks you to give something up, do so in faith, not fear. When the Father offers us the kingdom, we can lessen our grip on the things that lead to worry and anxiety.

Pause

Write down what you fear losing the most. Consider how these things may be treasures in your heart and how they might contribute to your anxiety.

Pray

Heavenly Father,

As I walk through each day, help me through the power of the Holy Spirit to hold things loosely, trusting that whatever you ask me to release is for my ultimate good and your greater glory. Let my security and joy come solely from your eternal presence and promises.

In the name of Jesus, who is my greatest treasure, I pray,
Amen.

Ponder

I choose to release my grip on worldly possessions and embrace the true security and fulfillment God offers when he is the treasure of my heart.

Memorize Matthew 6:19-21

> 19 Do not lay up for yourselves treasures on earth, where moth and rust destroy and where thieves break in and steal, 20 but lay up for yourselves treasures in heaven, where neither moth nor rust destroys and where thieves do not break in and steal. 21 For where your treasure is, there your heart will be also.

Day 02

Finding Contentment

— PHILIPPIANS 4:11–13

11 Not that I am speaking of being in
need, for I have learned in whatever
situation I am to be content. 12 I know
how to be brought low, and I know
how to abound. In any and every
circumstance, I have learned the secret
of facing plenty and hunger, abundance
and need. 13 I can do all things through
him who strengthens me.

Do you ever find yourself in the "one-day" mindset, believing that "one day I'll be out of debt," "one day I'll have enough money," "one day I'll be able to stop worrying about my investments," or "one day I'll finally be able to relax"?

We yearn for contentment, hoping to find it someday, but is it possible to experience contentment in every moment of every day? According to Paul, it is indeed possible. Our mistake lies in seeking contentment in the wrong places.

When our contentment depends on our circumstances, it will always be temporary because circumstances constantly change. During his lifetime, the Apostle Paul went from worldly success to the depths of poverty. He had been a well-respected Pharisee but became an imprisoned and impoverished follower of Christ. Despite all this, Paul writes in Philippians 4 that he had discovered the secret to contentment. **It was not in his circumstances but in the person and work of Jesus.**

When we take our eyes off our circumstances and place them on God as Paul did, it changes our perspective. We begin to see that nothing in this world—not money, success, status, people, possessions, or a booming economy—will ever bring lasting contentment. Only a deep, personal relationship with Jesus can offer what our souls long for.

Hebrews 13:5 encourages us to *"keep your life free from love of money, and be content with what you have, for he has said, 'I will never leave you nor forsake you.'"*

Let us find peace and contentment in the promise that God will never leave us nor forsake us, no matter how bleak our current situation may appear. May our lives be free from the love of money and full of the love of God—the treasure of our hearts and our strength to find peace and contentment in any circumstance.

Pause

List out the things that you are looking to "one day" provide you with contentment. Consider how even good things can become bad if they take the place of God in your heart.

Pray

Heavenly Father,

I acknowledge that true joy and peace cannot be found in the abundance of possessions or the things of this world. I turn my heart towards you, the eternal source of all goodness and peace. Teach me to find contentment in your presence, to treasure your unending love and grace in my life.

In Jesus' name, I pray,
Amen.

Ponder

My contentment and joy are not rooted in my circumstances but in the person and work of Jesus.

Continue to memorize Matthew 6:19-21

> 19 Do not lay up for yourselves treasures on earth, where moth and rust destroy and where thieves break in and steal, 20 but lay up for yourselves treasures in heaven, where neither moth nor rust destroys and where thieves do not break in and steal. 21 For where your treasure is, there your heart will be also.

Day 03

Incline My Heart

— PSALM 119:36–37

36 Incline my heart to your testimonies, and not to selfish gain!

37 Turn my eyes from looking at worthless things; and give me life in your ways.

In the hustle and grind of daily life, it's easy to get caught up in the vicious trap of anxiety if we continually go after selfish pursuits. The psalmist's plea for God to turn his heart toward his commands and away from selfish gain highlights a fundamental truth: *"Where your treasure is, there your heart will be also"* (Matthew 6:21).

The desire for *"selfish gain"* represents the countless distractions and temptations that can pull us away from God and push our focus onto ourselves. It is through this *"pursuit of the wind"* (Ecclesiastes 1:14) that we drive ourselves further and further into the pit of anxiety. Whether it's chasing success, happiness, or stability, these things are ultimately fleeting and incapable of satisfying the deepest longings of our hearts.

In contrast, God's Word is eternal and life-giving. By seeking God's guidance and prioritizing his will, we align ourselves with his purpose and experience true fulfillment.

Turning our eyes away from *"worthless things"* is a call to shift our focus from the temporary to the eternal. It's a complete reality shift that now sees the previous pursuits of life as utterly insufficient compared to what God has in store for us.

The famous evangelist and publisher D. L. Moody once said:

"Our greatest fear should not be of failure, but of succeeding at something that doesn't really matter."

As we continue to grow in our faith, may we continually ask God to direct our hearts toward his statutes and away from selfish pursuits. May we find our greatest joy and satisfaction in knowing him and living according to his Word. When we treasure God above all, we let go of this anxious pursuit of everything worldly and take hold of the richness of life centered on his eternal promises and love.

Pause

Create a "Treasure Jar" where you write down moments of God's faithfulness, answered prayers, or meaningful scripture passages on small pieces of paper. Reflect on these during tough times to remind yourself of God's eternal value over worldly distractions.

Pray

Heavenly Father,

Guide my steps and decisions so I may live according to your will. Fill me with a desire for your wisdom and a longing to know you more deeply. Protect me from the temptations of this world and remind me constantly that true fulfillment and joy come only from you.

In Jesus' name, I pray,
Amen.

Ponder

I will treasure God's eternal Word above all worldly gains, seeking his guidance and living according to his statutes for true fulfillment and joy.

Continue to memorize Matthew 6:19-21

> [19] Do not lay up for yourselves treasures on earth, where moth and rust destroy and where thieves break in and steal, [20] but lay up for yourselves treasures in heaven, where neither moth nor rust destroys and where thieves do not break in and steal. [21] For where your treasure is, there your heart will be also.

Light OVERCOMES *Darkness*

Day 04

The Eye Is the Lamp

— MATTHEW 6:22–23

Day 05

Called Out of Darkness

— 1 PETER 2:9

Day 06

Strength through Weakness

— 2 CORINTHIANS 12:10

Day 04

The Eye Is the Lamp

— MATTHEW 6:22–23

22 The eye is the lamp of the body. So,
if your eye is healthy, your whole body
will be full of light,
23 but if your eye
is bad, your whole body will be full of
darkness. If then the light in you is
darkness, how great is the darkness!

Jesus uses the metaphor of the eye being the lamp of the body to illustrate a deeper spiritual truth about how we perceive and interact with the world. The state of our "eye"—our heart's focus and priority—determines whether we live in light or darkness.

A healthy eye is focused on God and his righteousness. An "unhealthy" eye is distracted, divided, greedy, and darkened by worldly concerns. When our eyes become filled with the worry-inducing messages of this world, and we become obsessed with how we compare materially with others, our hearts risk drifting away from that which is good and true.

The problem with darkness is that if we look at it long enough, our eyes will begin to adjust to it, and it will eventually cease to look dark. The prophet Isaiah writes, *"Woe to those who call evil good and good evil, who put darkness for light and light for darkness, who put bitter for sweet and sweet for bitter!"* (Isaiah 5:20)

But there is good news. John 1:5 says, *"The light shines in the darkness, and the darkness has not overcome it."* Later, he reminds us, *"I have come into the world as light, so that whoever believes in me may not remain in darkness"* (John 12:46).

When we continue to live our lives focused on what the world tells us to concern ourselves with, it blinds us to the truth of God's purpose for our lives. Be aware of what your eyes are looking at. Don't let them adjust to the darkness, which produces worry, fear, and anxiety. Fix your eyes on Jesus, and you *"will not walk in darkness, but will have the light of life"* (John 8:12).

Pause

Take a moment to write down what your eyes are looking at each day. Circle the items on the list that lead to fear and anxiety. Consider any changes you need to make in light of this exercise.

Pray

Heavenly Father,

Help me to see the world through your eyes, focused on your kingdom and righteousness. Grant me the grace to let go of worldly distractions and selfishness. Keep my heart steadfast and my eyes ever focused on you.

I ask these things in the precious name of Jesus,
Amen.

Ponder

Memorize Matthew 6:22-23

> 22 The eye is the lamp of the body. So, if your eye is
> healthy, your whole body will be full of light, 23 but if
> your eye is bad, your whole body will be full of darkness.
> If then the light in you is darkness, how great is
> the darkness!

Day 05

Called Out of Darkness

— 1 PETER 2:9

9 But you are a chosen race, a royal
priesthood, a holy nation, a people
for his own possession, that you may
proclaim the excellencies of him who
called you out of darkness into his
marvelous light.

Fear and anxiety have the ability to obscure your identity. Worry clouds your day and can cause you to forget who you are as God's beloved. This chaos doesn't just disturb your peace; it hides a profound truth that should bring eternal comfort: You belong to the King of Kings.

One of the most powerful human needs is to belong. Peter addressed this desire in his letter to the scattered and persecuted Christians in Asia Minor.

To be a light in the darkness, you must know who—and whose—you are:

— **You are chosen.** As a member of the New Testament church, you are part of an extended family, chosen by name to follow the King of Kings.

— **You are part of a royal priesthood.** Jesus's perfect life, death, and resurrection restored the relationship between the Creator and his creation. In Christ, you can confidently approach, worship, and serve our holy God. You are a child of the King!

— **You are set apart.** As a follower of Jesus, you are part of God's covenantal promise, included in his plan to bless the world.

— **You are his possession.** Secured by mercy and sustained by grace, you are owned by the Lord. He will never leave you, forsake you, or let you go.

No matter the financial pressures that are upon you, they cannot overcome you, *"for he who is in you who is in you is greater than he who is in the world"* (1 John 4:4). Remember, you have been called out of darkness and into the light. In your challenges, invite the Holy Spirit to dispel any shadows of darkness in your life and rejoice in the truth of the light and knowledge that you belong to the Lord.

Pause

In what ways does worry cloud my identity as a child of God?

Read 2 Corinthians 4:16-18, 2 Corinthians 5:17, Galatians 2:20, and write out what these passages say about your identity in Christ.

Pray

Jesus,

You paid the ultimate price for me on the cross, and I belong to you. Because of your death and resurrection, I am chosen, I am a part of a royal priesthood, I am set apart, and I am your possession. May this knowledge empower me to live boldly and faithfully, serving as a beacon of your love and light in this world.

In your name, I pray,
Amen.

Ponder

I am a chosen, royal, and holy child of God, called out of darkness into his marvelous light, and no burden or worry can diminish the truth of who I am and whose I am.

Continue to memorize Matthew 6:22-23

> 22 The eye is the lamp of the body. So, if your eye is healthy, your whole body will be full of light, 23 but if your eye is bad, your whole body will be full of darkness. If then the light in you is darkness, how great is the darkness!

Day 06

Strength through Weakness

— 2 CORINTHIANS 12:10

10 For the sake of Christ, then, I am
content with weaknesses, insults,
hardships, persecutions, and
calamities. For when I am weak,
then I am strong.

Fear and anxiety can leave us feeling frail and weak. Financial worries begin to gnaw away at us as struggles and uncertainty abound—a feeling of darkness surrounds us.

In our state of helplessness, we are faced with a paradoxical truth—it is through our weaknesses that we become strong. Paul knew full well what it meant to be weak. He had a "thorn in his flesh" that he pleaded with God three times to remove. God's response was, *"My grace is sufficient for you, for my power is made perfect in weakness"* (2 Corinthians 12:9).

Are you calling upon God to remove a financial "thorn" in your life? May his grace be sufficient, for *"he gives power to the faint, and to him who has no might he increases strength"* (Isaiah 40:29).

Your Heavenly Father knows your struggles and invites you to bring them to him so that he can give you strength and be your strength! For his sake, will you let his power be made evident in your life through your weakness?

Rather than viewing financial difficulties as obstacles or sources of shame, we can begin to see them as opportunities through which God's power and grace can vividly shine. This perspective enables us to endure and overcome challenges in ways that highlight God's greatness.

If worries are consuming you and you're feeling depleted, remind yourself that God is with you to be your strength. Be *"strong and courageous. Do not be frightened, and do not be dismayed, for the LORD your God is with you wherever you go"* (Joshua 1:9).

Pause

What financial stress are you hiding so that you don't appear weak? How can God's strength be displayed in your life if you were to surrender your situation over to him?

Pray

Heavenly Father,

Help me to be strong and courageous, not dismayed by challenges, for you, Lord, are with me wherever I go. Let your strength shine brightest in my weakest moments, transforming my fears into testimonies of your faithfulness.

In the name of Jesus, I pray, and by the power of the Holy Spirit, Amen.

Ponder

I am strong in my weaknesses because God's grace is sufficient for me, and his power is perfected when I fully depend on him.

Continue to memorize Matthew 6:22-23

> 22 The eye is the lamp of the body. So, if your eye is healthy, your whole body will be full of light, 23 but if your eye is bad, your whole body will be full of darkness. If then the light in you is darkness, how great is the darkness!

CAN'T SERVE

God & Money

Day 07

Can't Serve God & Money

— MATTHEW 6:24

Day 08

More Than Enough

— JOHN 10:10

Day 09

Rest for Your Soul

— MATTHEW 11:28–30

Day 07

Can't Serve God & Money

— MATTHEW 6:24

24 No one can serve two masters, for either he will hate the one and love the other, or he will be devoted to the one and despise the other. You cannot serve God and money.

The human heart does not have the capacity for divided allegiances. Any attempt to serve two masters will eventually force us to choose which one we will follow.

When the Bible talks about money, it often represents more than mere currency; it symbolizes worldly values and pursuits that can lead one away from a God-centered life. Wealth, power, success, security, and all that the world deems essential can quickly become idols we serve, often without even realizing it.

Of course, money isn't evil in and of itself. It's a good gift from God that we can use as a tool to accomplish his purposes. But if the enemy can deceive us into believing that money can provide the identity and security that only God provides, money will enslave us and quickly draw our hearts away from God.

Larry Burkett articulated, *"The love of money is a form of idol worship, just as surely as the worship of pagan images. It is not the money that is the problem; it's the attitude toward it."*

We must choose whom we will serve, as Joshua 24:15 points out:

And if it is evil in your eyes to serve the LORD, choose this day whom you will serve, whether the gods your fathers served in the region beyond the River, or the gods of the Amorites in whose land you dwell. ***But as for me and my house, we will serve the LORD."***

Will you choose to serve the Lord? Will you trust him with your worries, struggles, and your future? In order to trust God, we must know him personally, and when we choose to serve him above all else, we find that he is our deepest source of joy and our ultimate treasure.

Pause

What most consumes your time, thoughts, and resources? Consider how serving these masters is contributing to your anxiety and how your heart can be redirected to love and serve God.

Time:

Thoughts:

Resources:

Pray

Heavenly Father,

I confess the times I have allowed the pursuit of money and possessions to cloud my vision and eclipse my devotion to you. I pray for a heart that desires you above all else. Grant me the wisdom to prioritize my life rightly, with you at the forefront.

In the name of Jesus, I pray,
Amen.

Ponder

I choose to serve the Lord wholeheartedly, trusting him above all worldly pursuits.

Memorize Matthew 6:24

> 24 No one can serve two masters, for either he will hate the one and love the other, or he will be devoted to the one and despise the other. You cannot serve God and money.

Day 08

More Than Enough

— JOHN 10:10

10 The thief comes only to steal and
kill and destroy. I came that they may
have life and have it abundantly.

In a world where things are often seen from a scarcity mindset, the idea of "not having enough" is anything but new. Since the creation of humanity, the enemy's purpose (the thief) has been to steal our peace, kill our joy, and destroy our trust in God's provision. The thief wants us to believe that we must constantly strive and hoard, fearing there won't be enough for tomorrow. This mindset traps us in a cycle of anxiety and distrust.

However, Jesus invites us into a different reality. He came so we might have life and have it to the fullest. God's abundance is a fundamental aspect of his character. His resources are limitless.

The very act of creation is a testament to God's boundless generosity. Every intricate detail of the universe, from the vast galaxies to the delicate petals of a flower, speaks of a Creator who delights in giving good gifts to his creation. He didn't create a barren world; he created a world teeming with beauty, a place where every element works together in harmony to sustain life.

So, what do we do when hardship, fear, and anxiety dominate our daily experiences? How do we shift our constant struggle for more to a joyous celebration of God's care and provision?

We look to Jesus, the embodiment of God's abundance, who lived generously despite facing adversity at every turn. When we choose to serve God over everything else, we are welcomed into a counter-cultural narrative of abundance that invites us to trust that with God, there will always be **more than enough**.

Pause

Consider what God has provided for you today, this month, and this year. Reflect on Psalm 23 and be reminded that you lack nothing with the Lord as your shepherd.

Pray

Dear Heavenly Father,

In your loving mercy, open my eyes to the beauty and possibility of a life lived in your abundance, where scarcity has no hold, and your love reigns supreme. May I walk confidently, knowing I am a cherished guest at your table, where there is always more than enough.

In the name of Jesus, I pray,
Amen.

Ponder

In trusting God's endless generosity, I reject the fear of scarcity and embrace a life of abundance, confident that there is always more than enough with God.

Continue to memorize Matthew 6:24

> 24 No one can serve two masters, for either he will hate the one and love the other, or he will be devoted to the one and despise the other. You cannot serve God and money.

Day 09

Rest for Your Soul

— MATTHEW 11:28–30

28 Come to me, all who labor and are
heavy laden, and I will give you rest.
29 Take my yoke upon you, and learn
from me, for I am gentle and lowly in
heart, and you will find rest for your
souls. 30 For my yoke is easy, and my
burden is light.

In Jesus' day, some of the Pharisees were guilty of burdening the Jewish people with numerous requirements to earn God's favor. Although intended to help people obey the law (Torah), these requirements were a heavy yoke—a mechanism used to connect oxen, representing weighty, hard work.

Today, our burdens may differ, but we often strive to earn God's favor and others' approval through our actions, especially in financial matters. Questions such as *"Am I doing this right?"* or *"Am I giving enough?"* can lead to anxiety and a feeling of burden as we try to be good stewards.

Scripture teaches us that our right standing with God isn't based on our actions but by grace through faith in Jesus (Ephesians 2:8-9). He fully paid our sin debt and invites us to stop striving and come to him for rest. This rest alleviates the anxiety of trying to earn God's approval.

When we stop striving and place our trust in Jesus, the Holy Spirit comes to dwell within us. This life-giving relationship leads us to embrace Jesus' easy yoke, trusting his ways are higher and better than ours. This doesn't eliminate life's burdens but relieves the pressure of bearing them on our own, knowing we can rely on God's strength.

In faith, we say *"Yes, Lord,"* out of joyful obedience, not anxious obligation, trusting him with every outcome. Through Jesus' work on the cross and the Spirit's work in us, we look forward to hearing *"Well done, good and faithful servant"* and entering into the joy of our true master.

Pause

Write this quote from Philip Yancey where you will see it every day and reflect on this truth daily:

"Grace means there is nothing I can do to make God love me more, and nothing I can do to make God love me less." – Philip Yancey

Write down any examples of how you may be trying to earn God's favor through your financial decisions.

Pray

Lord Jesus,

My soul comes to you weary and burdened, seeking the rest only you can provide. Teach me to lay down the weight of my worries and fears about the future at your feet. Help me to walk in your paths, where the burden is light and the journey is filled with grace.

In your holy name, I pray,
Amen.

Ponder

I can lay down my burdens at the feet of Jesus, taking his light and easy yoke upon me to find rest for my soul and learn from his gentle and humble heart.

Continue to memorize Matthew 6:24

> 24 No one can serve two masters, for either he will hate the one and love the other, or he will be devoted to the one and despise the other. You cannot serve God and money.

DON'T BE ANXIOUS *About Your Life*

Day 10
Do Not Be Anxious

— MATTHEW 6:25

Day 11
The Peace of God

— PHILIPPIANS 4:6–7

Day 12
Help in Time of Need

— HEBREWS 4:15–16

Day 10

Do Not Be Anxious

— MATTHEW 6:25

25 Therefore I tell you, do not be
anxious about your life, what you will
eat or what you will drink, nor about
your body, what you will put on. Is
not life more than food, and the body
more than clothing?

Anxiety is a universal human condition—the fear that things won't go well. We watch sporting events, elections, our bank accounts, and our investment portfolios with much anxiety. If we knew the outcomes beforehand, we would not be anxious.

However, in an effort to control our circumstances, we worry about uncertain outcomes, as if we are putting an emotional downpayment on something that may never happen.

The late Billy Graham once said:

"Some people spend so much time worrying about what might happen that they never enjoy what is happening [now]... Today is the tomorrow you worried about yesterday."

Jesus' command to refrain from anxiety goes beyond urging people to remain calm; rather, it reveals the very foundation of our security. It requires that our security not lie in our wealth or planning but in our abiding relationship with him. It reassures us that God is completely in control of all of our circumstances.

To overcome anxiety, we must grow in faith. To have faith, we must not try harder but surrender more. From big decisions to daily needs, we can put them in God's hands. If that seems scary or even impossible, it may stem from the fact that we can't trust someone we don't know.

You would never give your bank credentials to a stranger because you don't know them and can't trust them. Similarly, you can't trust God if you don't know him personally and intimately. As you grow in your relationship with him through prayer, the reading of his Word, and fellowship with the body of Christ, you can begin to trust him to meet your needs for today and tomorrow.

Pause

Recite the famous Serenity Prayer, thought to be written by Dr. Reinhold Niebuhr:

God, grant me the serenity
to accept the things I cannot change,
the courage to change the things I can,
and the wisdom to know the difference.
Living one day at a time,
enjoying one moment at a time;
accepting hardship as a pathway to peace;
taking, as Jesus did,
this sinful world as it is,
not as I would have it;
trusting that You will make all things right
if I surrender to Your will;
so that I may be reasonably happy in this life
and supremely happy with You forever in the next.

Amen.

Pray

Heavenly Father,

When I feel overwhelmed by the unknown, guide my heart to rest in your promises. Help me release my grip on the things I cannot control and place them in your loving hands. Strengthen my relationship with you so I may know and trust you more intimately.

I pray this in the name of Jesus,
Amen.

Ponder

To overcome anxiety, I must grow in faith and surrender control to God, recognizing that my security lies in a personal and intimate relationship with him.

Memorize Matthew 6:25

> 25 Therefore I tell you, do not be anxious about your life, what you will eat or what you will drink, nor about your body, what you will put on. Is not life more than food, and the body more than clothing?

Day 11

The Peace of God

— PHILIPPIANS 4:6–7

6 do not be anxious about anything,
but in everything by prayer and
supplication with thanksgiving let
your requests be made known to
God. 7 And the peace of God, which
surpasses all understanding, will
guard your hearts and your minds in
Christ Jesus.

When uncertainty surrounds your financial situation, it can lead to paralyzing fear and anxiety. Your heart rate elevates, your thoughts become clouded, and endless questions consume your mind as uncertainty leaves you in a bottomless pit of worry.

Yet, Paul instructs us to *"not be anxious about anything."* The church at Philippi, to whom Paul wrote this, was no stranger to anxiety. Though they were under extreme oppression daily, Paul provided them and us with critical instructions on how we can overcome our anxious thoughts and deepest financial fears.

Rather than dwelling on your circumstances, no matter how difficult they may appear, make your requests known to God. Bring your anxieties, fears, and problems to him. And do so in a posture of thanksgiving. Yes, thanksgiving! Give him thanks for the ways he has provided for you in the past. Give thanks that he has overcome the world and is ultimately victorious over the most dire and dark situations.

He will then fill you with a peace that surpasses all understanding. It's inexplicable. You've likely seen people who are at peace when it seems like everything around them is crashing in. It's a sustaining, prevailing peace that doesn't negate the circumstance—it empowers you to endure it. Peace comes from trusting in God, and when you trust him, he will guard your heart and mind in Christ Jesus.

A dark cloud of anxiety may be all around you. Don't minimize your fears and anxious thoughts. Bring them to God—honestly and transparently. Give him thanks because you trust him with the outcomes, knowing he *"works for the good of those who love him, who have been called according to his purpose"* (Romans 8:28 NIV).

Pause

Reflect on the times in your life when God has provided for you in a time of need and great anxiety. Write him a thank you note for those moments.

Pray

Heavenly Father,

Fill me with your peace—a peace that surpasses all understanding. Help me to trust in your goodness and your ability to work all things together for my good. Let your peace sustain me and help me endure every trial with a confident heart.

In Jesus' name, I pray,
Amen.

Ponder

I trust in God's provision and peace, bringing my anxieties to him with thanksgiving, knowing he is in control and works all things for my good.

Continue to memorize Matthew 6:25

> 25 Therefore I tell you, do not be anxious about your life, what you will eat or what you will drink, nor about your body, what you will put on. Is not life more than food, and the body more than clothing?

Day 12

Help in Time of Need

— HEBREWS 4:15–16

15 For we do not have a high priest
who is unable to sympathize with our
weaknesses, but one who in every
respect has been tempted as we are,
yet without sin. 16 Let us then with
confidence draw near to the throne of
grace, that we may receive mercy and
find grace to help in time of need.

When faced with financial struggles or anxieties, we may feel as though God is distant and unable to relate to our situations. However, the very incarnation of Christ is a reminder that God knows our limitations. Psalm 103:14 reminds us that *"he knows our frame; he remembers that we are dust."*

Jesus can empathize with our struggles and hardships because he, himself, experienced them being fully God and fully man. He was in great agony as he prayed on the Mount of Olives, his sweat becoming *"like great drops of blood"* (Luke 22:44). He experienced temptation, hunger, exhaustion, frustration, and even poverty. Like us, Jesus needed money to live. He was financially supported by Mary Magdalene, Joanna, and Susanna (Luke 8:1-3). He knowingly entrusted those resources to a thief, Judas, whose love for money eventually led to his betrayal of Jesus.

He faced more suffering than any of us could ever bear in one lifetime, yet he did all of this without sin. This means he not only understands our weaknesses but also provides the perfect source of help to overcome them. His sinlessness does not make him less empathetic; rather, it underscores his unique ability to offer us both compassion and the strength to persevere.

In our moments of financial uncertainty, let us remember that we are never alone. God is with us. He invites us to bring our burdens to him, to receive his mercy, and to find grace to help in our time of need. We can rest assured that our Savior understands our financial struggles, sympathizes with our weaknesses, and is *"our refuge and strength, a very present help in trouble"* (Psalm 46:1).

Pause

Write a letter to Jesus, expressing your struggles and asking for his understanding and help. Pour out your heart, knowing that he can empathize with your weaknesses and offer you compassion.

Pray

Lord Jesus,

You know my weaknesses and the burdens I carry, and you offer the perfect help to overcome them. I come boldly to your throne, seeking your mercy and grace that I need in times of trouble.

It's in your name that I pray,
Amen.

Ponder

God understands my struggles and is always with me, offering his mercy and grace in my times of need.

Continue to memorize Matthew 6:25

> 25 Therefore I tell you, do not be anxious about your life, what you will eat or what you will drink, nor about your body, what you will put on. Is not life more than food, and the body more than clothing?

LOOK AT THE BIRDS,

Consider The Lilies

Day 13

Look at the Birds

— MATTHEW 6:26–30

Day 14

Become Like a Child

— LUKE 18:17

Day 15

God Is Our Provider

— DEUTERONOMY 8:17–18

Day 13

Look at the Birds

— MATTHEW 6:26–30

26 Look at the birds of the air: they neither sow
nor reap nor gather into barns, and yet your
heavenly Father feeds them. Are you not of more
value than they? 27 And which of you by being
anxious can add a single hour to his span of
life? 28 And why are you anxious about clothing?
Consider the lilies of the field, how they grow:
they neither toil nor spin, 29 yet I tell you, even
Solomon in all his glory was not arrayed like
one of these. 30 But if God so clothes the grass
of the field, which today is alive and tomorrow
is thrown into the oven, will he not much more
clothe you, O you of little faith?

"Look at the birds of the air." There is something to be said for actually looking at the birds God has made. Slow down long enough to observe their behavior. See how they sit on a branch, peck at the ground, and gracefully glide through the air. There is beauty in the simplicity of how they live, and yet, you are more valuable to God than the birds.

Matthew 10:29-31 says:

"Are not two sparrows sold for a penny? And not one of them will fall to the ground apart from your Father. But even the hairs of your head are all numbered. Fear not, therefore; you are of more value than many sparrows."

"Consider the lilies of the field." Flowers don't strive to be beautiful. They grow slowly and patiently, dependent on God's provision of soil, rain, and sunlight. They are vulnerable yet flourish—radiating more beauty than anything King Solomon ever wore.

If God takes care of the birds of the air and the flowers of the fields, won't he take care of you? Aren't you, made in his image, of more value to him?

If we believe God loves and cares for us, then there will be no doubt that he is capable of helping us in our times of need. Having faith in God and his ability to provide does not mean he will give you whatever you **want**. But he will supply your every **need**.

Are you anxious? Look at the sparrows and consider the flowers. Observe their dependence on God, and let them remind you of how much more your Father loves and cares for you.

Pause

Go outside and observe God's creation. Look at the birds and the flowers and remember that just as God provides for them, he will provide for you.

Pray

Heavenly Father,

As I reflect on the birds of the air and the lilies of the field, I'm reminded of your meticulous attention to detail and your deep love for me. Help me remember that I am of great value to you and that I can trust you to provide for my needs.

In the name of Jesus, I pray,
Amen.

Ponder

I don't need to worry about my needs, for just as God cares for the birds and the lilies, he values me even more, so I will trust in his faithful provision.

Memorize Matthew 6:26-30

> [26] Look at the birds of the air: they neither sow nor reap
> nor gather into barns, and yet your heavenly Father feeds
> them. Are you not of more value than they? [27] And which
> of you by being anxious can add a single hour to his
> span of life? [28] And why are you anxious about clothing?
> Consider the lilies of the field, how they grow: they
> neither toil nor spin, [29] yet I tell you, even Solomon in all
> his glory was not arrayed like one of these. [30] But if God
> so clothes the grass of the field, which today is alive and
> tomorrow is thrown into the oven, will he not much more
> clothe you, O you of little faith?

Day 14

Become Like a Child

— LUKE 18:17

17 Truly, I say to you, whoever does not
receive the kingdom of God like a child
shall not enter it.

When we consider Luke 18:17, we see Jesus holding up children as exemplars of the humble posture necessary to receive the kingdom of God. But what does this mean for us, especially in our struggles with financial stress? Why would he tell us to look to children as our example? Young children don't provide for themselves, they need help frequently (even when they don't want it), and they're not preoccupied with the future. However, that's precisely what Jesus is getting at. The very weaknesses that we often see in kids are actually strengths in the eyes of Jesus.

Children naturally trust and depend on their parents for everything they need. They do not worry about where their next meal will come from, whether they will have clothes for tomorrow, or if their house will be there for them when they get back from somewhere. Similarly, Jesus calls us to trust God completely, recognizing our dependence on him for all aspects of our lives. This childlike trust means believing that God is our provider and protector, even when circumstances feel precarious.

By calling us to become like children, Jesus does not suggest we remain immature or naive. As Paul reminds us in 1 Corinthians 13:11:

"When I was a child, I spoke like a child, I thought like a child, I reasoned like a child. When I became a man, I gave up childish ways."

In Luke 18, Jesus is referring to the qualities of trust, humility, simplicity, and recognized dependence that characterize a child's relationship with their parent. These qualities are essential for entering and experiencing the kingdom of God.

Even when we must continue to fulfill our responsibilities as adults, we can approach our challenges as children of our Heavenly Father, knowing that our needs will always be met in him.

Pause

Identify the worries in your life that you struggle releasing to God. Consciously let go of those worries by opening your hands to reach for God, like a child reaching toward a loving parent.

Pray

Heavenly Father,

Help me to let go of my need for control, my desire to foresee every outcome, and my tendency to rely on my own plans. Teach me to trust you fully, as a child trusts a loving parent, without fear or reservation.

In Jesus' name,
Amen.

Ponder

I will become like a child, trusting in God's sovereignty and care without needing to control or foresee every outcome, finding peace in his mysterious ways.

Continue to memorize Matthew 6:26-30

> 26 Look at the birds of the air: they neither sow nor reap
> nor gather into barns, and yet your heavenly Father feeds
> them. Are you not of more value than they? 27 And which
> of you by being anxious can add a single hour to his
> span of life? 28 And why are you anxious about clothing?
> Consider the lilies of the field, how they grow: they
> neither toil nor spin, 29 yet I tell you, even Solomon in all
> his glory was not arrayed like one of these. 30 But if God
> so clothes the grass of the field, which today is alive and
> tomorrow is thrown into the oven, will he not much more
> clothe you, O you of little faith?

Day 15

God Is Our Provider

— DEUTERONOMY 8:17–18

17 Beware lest you say in your heart,
“My power and the might of my hand
have gotten me this wealth.” 18 You
shall remember the LORD your God,
for it is he who gives you power to
get wealth, that he may confirm
his covenant that he swore to your
fathers, as it is this day.

In the midst of our busy lives, with looming deadlines and increasing responsibilities, it's easy to see our work and the money it brings in as the only way to provide for ourselves and our families. However, Scripture gently redirects our gaze to a comforting truth: God is our provider, and through our work, he equips us to be stewards of his abundance.

In the context of Deuteronomy 8:17–18, Moses addresses the second generation of Israelites wandering through the desert on the way to the promised land—a land described as *"flowing with milk and honey"* (Exodus 3:8). Prosperity, wealth, and success were imminent, which opened up opportunities for temptation to present itself in the form of arrogance and self-reliance. In these verses, Moses encourages the Israelites to be humble and remember that God not only provides wealth but is the very source of our talents, energy, and opportunities. Acknowledging this humbles us and fills us with gratitude towards God, who chooses to involve us in his divine economy.

Understanding that God is our provider liberates us from the anxiety and pressure of feeling solely responsible for our financial security. It allows us to approach our work with purpose and gratitude, seeing our daily tasks as opportunities to witness God's provision in action. This perspective doesn't diminish the value of hard work but enriches it with meaning as we sit in awe of God's generous provision.

As you lean into the truth that God is your provider, may your work become an act of worship, a grateful response to the one who lovingly supplies *"every need of yours according to his riches in glory in Christ Jesus"* (Philippians 4:19).

Pause

Write down the opportunities and unique abilities God has given you, and reflect on how these are not your own doing but gifts from him.

Pray

Father God,

I ask for the faith to trust you as my provider, releasing the burdens of self-sufficiency and control. Help me find the freedom to pursue my work joyfully, seeing it as your provision and care.

I offer this prayer in the name of Jesus Christ, through whom I have received the greatest provision—salvation and life everlasting.
Amen.

Ponder

God is my ultimate provider, giving me the ability and privilege of stewarding his abundance with humility and gratitude.

Continue to memorize Matthew 6:26-30

> 26 Look at the birds of the air: they neither sow nor reap
> nor gather into barns, and yet your heavenly Father feeds
> them. Are you not of more value than they? 27 And which
> of you by being anxious can add a single hour to his
> span of life? 28 And why are you anxious about clothing?
> Consider the lilies of the field, how they grow: they
> neither toil nor spin, 29 yet I tell you, even Solomon in all
> his glory was not arrayed like one of these. 30 But if God
> so clothes the grass of the field, which today is alive and
> tomorrow is thrown into the oven, will he not much more
> clothe you, O you of little faith?

holy bible

SEEK FIRST

The Kingdom of God

Day 16

Seek First

— MATTHEW 6:31–33

Day 17

Set Your Mind on Things Above

— COLOSSIANS 3:2

Day 18

Hidden Treasure

— MATTHEW 13:44

Day 16

Seek First

— MATTHEW 6:31–33

31 Therefore do not be anxious, saying,
"What shall we eat?" or "What shall
we drink?" or "What shall we wear?"
32 For the Gentiles seek after all these
things, and your heavenly Father
knows that you need them all. 33 But
seek first the kingdom of God and his
righteousness, and all these things
will be added to you.

God knows exactly what you need—in fact, he knows what you need better than you do. That's why Jesus has given you the key to unlocking the heavy, restrictive, and painful chains of anxiety: *"Seek first the kingdom of God and his righteousness."*

The Gentiles (unbelievers) thought they could relieve their anxiety through accumulation and consumption. Their eyes were fixed on the things of this world. They were worried: *"What if I won't have enough?" "What will others think of me?"*

We may face similar worries, but Jesus invites his followers to stop pursuing the things of this world and prioritize a relationship with him above all else. This does not mean we neglect our responsibilities; rather, everything in our lives is put into proper order when we seek him first.

You may recall the "order of operations" from algebra class—PEMDAS, which stands for parenthesis, exponents, multiplication, division, addition, and subtraction. When solving a math problem, we go from left to right using PEMDAS. Let's give it a try: $4 + 5 \times 2 = ??$

You'll get the wrong answer if you don't follow the order of operations. Using PEMDAS, we do multiplication first (5×2), then addition ($4 + 10$) to find that the answer is 14. If you thought the answer was 18, you got the wrong answer because you did the operations out of order.

Oftentimes, you may wonder why you are anxious and worried about things that are out of your control. Take a step back and evaluate what you are prioritizing. Are things in your life out of order?

As we seek God's kingdom and righteousness first, Jesus promises that all our needs will be met. It doesn't mean we won't face challenges, but we can trust God to sustain us through them and provide what we need to fulfill his purposes.

Pause

Ask the Holy Spirit to show you some ways you can order your daily life in a way that puts him first. Write them down, and then ask the Holy Spirit to help you do them.

Pray

Father God,

Thank you for knowing me and loving me. Help me to seek first your kingdom and your righteousness. Take first place in my heart and my life. I submit my fears and anxieties to you; I believe you will provide what I need.

In Jesus' name, I pray,
Amen.

Ponder

When I seek first the kingdom of God and his righteousness, I can trust that all my needs will be met as I focus on his eternal promises.

Memorize Matthew 6:31-33

> 31 Therefore do not be anxious, saying, "What shall we eat?" or "What shall we drink?" or "What shall we wear?"
> 32 For the Gentiles seek after all these things, and your heavenly Father knows that you need them all. 33 But seek first the kingdom of God and his righteousness, and all these things will be added to you.

Day 17

Set Your Mind on Things Above

— COLOSSIANS 3:2

2 Set your minds on things
that are above, not on things
that are on earth.

When our minds are consumed with the things of the world, it brings about anxiety because the things of this world will never satisfy our deepest desires. But to set our mind on things above is a radical reorientation of our thoughts and priorities rooted in our new identity in Christ. As believers, we have been raised with Christ (Colossians 3:1) and are now citizens of heaven (Philippians 3:20). Our lives are hidden with Christ in God (Colossians 3:3), and we are called to live in light of this truth. As Helen Howarth Lemmel's 1922 hymn *Turn Your Eyes Upon Jesus* says:

"Turn your eyes upon Jesus,
Look full in His wonderful face,
And the things of earth will grow strangely dim,
In the light of His glory and grace."

Turning our eyes upon Jesus doesn't mean we withdraw from the world or neglect our responsibilities; rather, we see the world differently. The Apostle Paul reminds us to *"look not to the things that are seen but to the things that are unseen. For the things that are seen are transient, but the things that are unseen are eternal"* (2 Corinthians 4:18).

When we live with an eternal perspective, we recognize that our current troubles are temporary. In contrast, the things above—God's kingdom and his love—are eternal and unchanging.

As we focus on heavenly realities, we experience the peace and joy that come from living in alignment with God's eternal purposes. Let us commit to fixing our eyes on Jesus, the founder and perfecter of our faith (Hebrews 12:2), and live as citizens of heaven, bringing glory to God in all we do.

Pause

Listen to the *Turn Your Eyes to Jesus* hymn on a music streaming service and recite these words throughout your day today:

"Turn your eyes upon Jesus,
Look full in his wonderful face,
And the things of earth will grow strangely dim,
In the light of his glory and grace."

Pray

Lord Jesus,

Help me to fix my eyes on you and set my mind on heavenly things. Fill my heart with your peace and joy, and remind me of the eternal truths that bring true fulfillment. Guide me to live each day for your glory, trusting in your unchanging love.

I pray this in your name and by the power of the Holy Spirit,
Amen.

Ponder

By fixing my eyes on Jesus and living with an eternal perspective, I recognize the temporary nature of my troubles and the unchanging nature of God's kingdom and love.

Continue to memorize Matthew 6:31-33

> 31 Therefore do not be anxious, saying, "What shall we eat?" or "What shall we drink?" or "What shall we wear?"
> 32 For the Gentiles seek after all these things, and your heavenly Father knows that you need them all. 33 But seek first the kingdom of God and his righteousness, and all these things will be added to you.

Day 18

Hidden Treasure

— MATTHEW 13:44

44 The kingdom of heaven is like
treasure hidden in a field, which a man
found and covered up. Then in his joy
he goes and sells all that he has and
buys that field.

Imagine stumbling upon a treasure so valuable that it eclipses everything you own. This is the image Jesus paints in Matthew 13:44. The kingdom of heaven is like this treasure—immeasurable, life-changing, and worth the ultimate sacrifice.

The man in the parable recognizes the unparalleled worth of the treasure. In his joy, he willingly sells all he has to acquire it. This joy is key. The sacrifice he makes isn't burdensome; it's a response to the immense value of what he has found.

In 2 Corinthians 8:1-5, we see a group of believers, the Macedonian churches, that had discovered the hidden treasure of God's kingdom. Their financial decisions didn't make much sense to the world around them, which is why Paul used their story as an example to encourage generosity in the church at Corinth.

Despite their extreme poverty, the Macedonians gave generously and joyfully, considering it a privilege to reflect God's love and grace to fellow believers in Jerusalem who were financially struggling. This is what happens when Christians are captivated by the upside-down nature of God's kingdom. They release their grip on material things to take hold of the kingdom treasure before them.

Jesus calls us to see his kingdom with the same clarity and joy. To seek God's kingdom means recognizing its supreme worth and prioritizing it above all else. It involves a willingness to let go of earthly attachments, trusting that what we gain in return far surpasses any sacrifice.

When the worries and anxieties of this world consume us, we are tempted to look to the world for answers, not realizing the greatest treasure is hidden right in front of us. And when we seek him with all of our heart, he promises that we will find him (Jeremiah 29:13).

Pause

Is there anything in your life right now preventing you from fully pursuing the kingdom of heaven? Bring those things to Jesus. Ask for his guidance and that he be the treasure of your heart.

Pray

Heavenly Father,

Help me to seek your kingdom like the man who found a hidden treasure in a field. Let my joy be found in your grace. Prepare my heart to let go of the desire for earthly accumulation so that you may be the sole treasure of my heart.

In the name of Jesus, I pray,
Amen.

Ponder

My hope and joy are found in eternal treasures rather than temporal solutions.

Continue to memorize Matthew 6:31-33

> 31 Therefore do not be anxious, saying, "What shall we eat?" or "What shall we drink?" or "What shall we wear?"
> 32 For the Gentiles seek after all these things, and your heavenly Father knows that you need them all. 33 But
> seek first the kingdom of God and his righteousness, and all these things will be added to you.

DON'T BE ANXIOUS

About Tomorrow

Day 19

Don't Be Anxious about Tomorrow

— MATTHEW 6:34

Day 20

Hopeful Plans

— PROVERBS 3:5–6

Day 21

Even If

— ISAIAH 41:10

Day 19

Don't Be Anxious about Tomorrow

— MATTHEW 6:34

34 Therefore do not be anxious about
tomorrow, for tomorrow will be
anxious for itself. Sufficient for the day
is its own trouble.

Many of our anxious thoughts might be driven by the financial uncertainty of tomorrow. Anxiety is often rooted in something out of our control, and we try to do everything we can to reach for the strings around us to puppeteer our way through life.

Jesus reminds us how futile this is in Matthew 6:27, *"And which of you by being anxious can add a single hour to his span of life?"*

Worrying does not change the outcome or extend one's life; it only adds unnecessary stress and detracts from one's trust in God. When we focus too much on the future, we can become overwhelmed and miss the opportunities and blessings of today. Well-known Holocaust survivor Corrie Ten Boom once said:

"Worry does not empty tomorrow of its sorrow; it empties today of its strength."

To experience God's peace, we must accept that no one knows what tomorrow holds, except for the one who holds it—God.

A comforting truth to always remember when we're anxious about tomorrow is that God knows where we've been, where we are, and where we're headed. God isn't confined by time (Revelation 1:4).

When we understand that God is outside of time itself, we recognize that time is something God has created. Because he created time, he isn't subject to its limitations. He is sovereign over every aspect of his creation, *"sustaining all things by his powerful word"* (Hebrews 1:3 NIV). Living with the knowledge that God has been and always will be on the throne (Psalm 45:6) reassures us that he has everything under control. Whatever we face in the days ahead, let us remember that we don't need to be anxious about tomorrow, for God is already there.

Pause

Write down all the things in the future that are creating a sense of fear and anxiety. Then, take a moment to relinquish each one to the Lord, and do this continuously as needed.

Pray

Lord God,

Your Word reminds me that worrying cannot add a single hour to my life. Help me to release my anxieties into your hands, knowing that you hold my past, present, and future. Teach me to live in the present, appreciating the blessings you have given me today.

I pray this in Jesus' name,
Amen.

Ponder

I can trust in God's sovereignty and let go of the anxiety about the future to embrace the peace and blessings of today.

Memorize Matthew 6:34

> 34 Therefore do not be anxious about tomorrow, for tomorrow will be anxious for itself. Sufficient for the day is its own trouble.

Day 20

Hopeful Plans

— PROVERBS 3:5–6

5 Trust in the LORD with all your
heart, and do not lean on your own
understanding.
6 In all your ways acknowledge him,
and he will make straight your paths.

Planning for the future is an essential aspect of life. From daily activities to long-term goals, we make plans for our spending, saving, employment, raising children, and retirement. But the critical question is: Are you planning out of fear or hope?

Fearful planners rely on their own understanding, driven by selfish desires and impulses rather than trusting in the Lord. Their plans are filled with worry and anxiety as they attempt to predict and control the future diligently.

Hopeful planners trust the Lord wholeheartedly and involve him in their planning. They are wise and knowledgeable, while they recognize their limitations and believe that God's ways are higher and better (Isaiah 55:8-9). They put their plans in God's hands, trusting that it is ultimately his purposes that will stand (Proverbs 19:21).

A fearful planner makes their plans without considering God, while a hopeful planner acknowledges that God directs their steps. James 4:13-15 tells us:

"Come now, you who say, 'Today or tomorrow we will go into such a town and spend a year there and trade and make a profit'—yet you do not know what tomorrow will bring. What is your life? For you are a mist that appears for a little time and then vanishes. Instead you ought to say, 'If the Lord wills, we will live and do this or that.'"

Planning helps us reach goals and take precautions for the challenges we will face, but we must commit our plans to the Lord and allow his plans to be established through us (Proverbs 16:3).

Pause

When you think about the future (retirement, education, career, housing, etc.), do you make plans from a place of hope or fear? How can you turn your fearful plans into hopeful plans?

Pray

Heavenly Father,

I confess that too often, I have planned out of fear, relying on my understanding and being driven by anxiety. Help me to plan with faith, knowing that you are with me and that you are good. Teach me to commit my plans to you and trust that you will establish them according to your will.

In Jesus' name, I pray,
Amen.

Ponder

I commit to being a hopeful planner, trusting in the Lord's wisdom over my own, and acknowledging him in every aspect of my life to ensure my paths are made straight and true.

Continue to memorize Matthew 6:34

> 34 Therefore do not be anxious about tomorrow, for tomorrow will be anxious for itself. Sufficient for the day is its own trouble.

Day 21

Even If

— ISAIAH 41:10

10 fear not, for I am with you;
be not dismayed, for I am your God;
I will strengthen you, I will help you,
I will uphold you with my righteous right hand.

One of the enemy's favorite tools for discouraging Christians is the question, "What if...?" "What if" questions lead right down the road to fear.

Maybe you've asked one of these recently:
— *"What if I lose my job?"*
— *"What if I don't have enough money for retirement?"*
— *"What if something bad happens to me or my loved ones?"*

In moments of uncertainty, we're faced with a choice: to succumb to fear and anxiety or to trust in God's provision. In other words, we can change our *"What if"* questions to *"Even if"* statements.

A profound example of unwavering faith under dire circumstances is found in the book of Daniel, where Shadrach, Meshach, and Abednego face a literal firestorm of persecution. These three young men, captives in Babylon, stood firm in their faith despite the threat of death in a blazing furnace—a punishment for refusing to worship an idol. Yet, they emerged unscathed, a testament to God's miraculous intervention. Before their ordeal, they declared to King Nebuchadnezzar:

"If the God we serve exists, then he can rescue us from the furnace of blazing fire, and he can rescue us from the power of you, the king. But ***even if*** *he does not rescue us, we want you as king to know that we will not serve your gods or worship the gold statue you set up"*
(Daniel 3:17-18 CSB).

Their faith acknowledged God's power to save while accepting his sovereignty, even if it meant not being delivered from hardship. Their trust wasn't conditional on the outcome but rooted in God's character.

In moments of financial anxiety, you can embrace that same trust. In Christ, you can avoid the *"What-if"* mentality and trust God will be your strength and help, **even if** things don't go according to your plans.

Pause

Write out some "What if" scenarios that you are struggling with right now. Once you're done writing those out, cross out the "What if" and replace them with "Even if." This will help you to trust in God even when your worst fears are realized.

Pray

Heavenly Father,

In moments of financial anxiety, I often ask, "What if?" and allow fear to take hold. Lord, help me shift my mindset from "What if" to "Even if." Even if I face financial uncertainty, loss, or hardship, I trust that you are with me.

In Christ's name, my all-sufficient peace, I pray,
Amen.

Ponder

My foundation isn't shaken even if I face challenges and uncertainties because I trust God's provision and sovereignty.

Continue to memorize Matthew 6:34

> 34 Therefore do not be anxious about tomorrow, for tomorrow will be anxious for itself. Sufficient for the day is its own trouble.

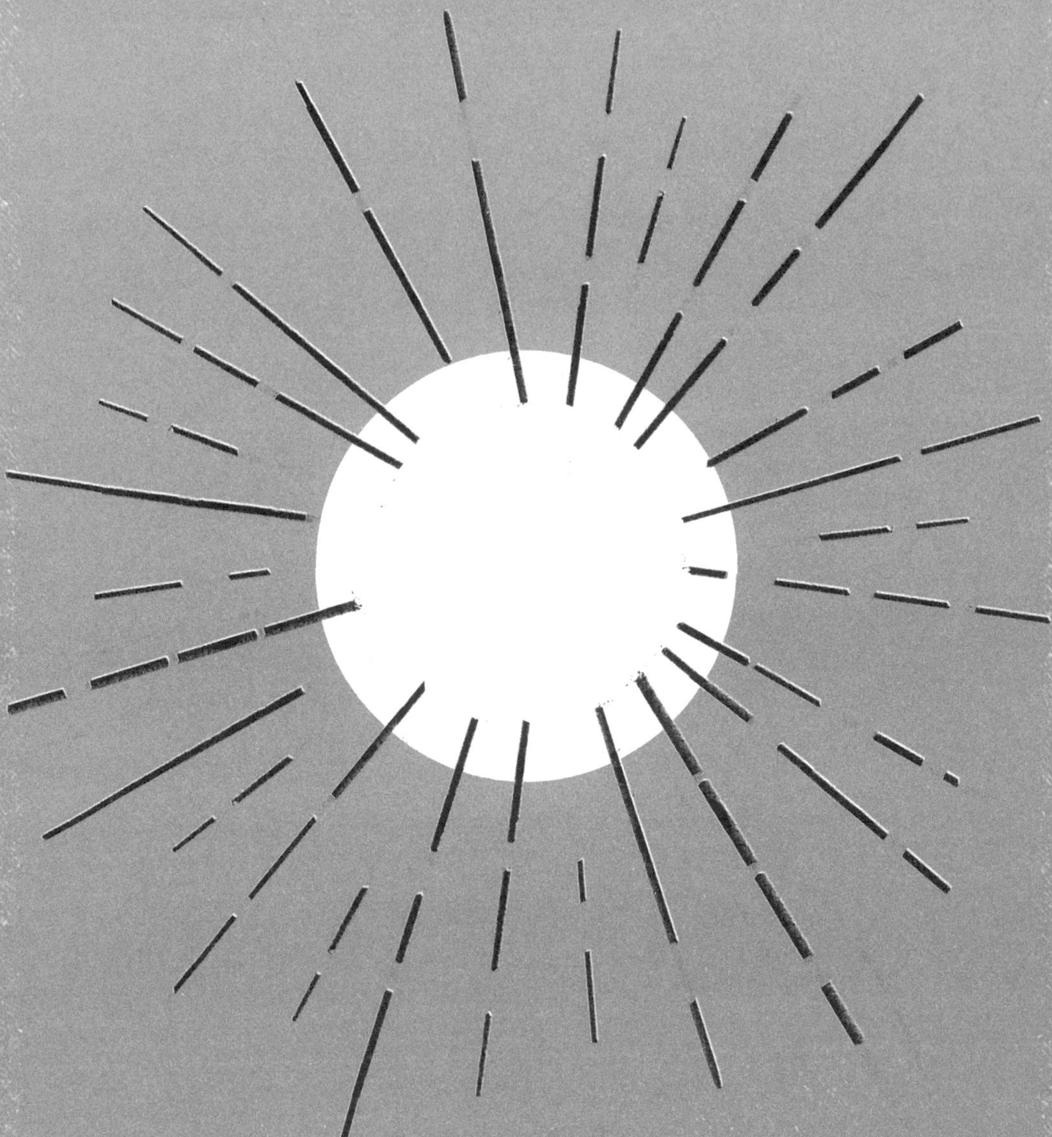

Reflection

As we come to a close on this devotional and reflect on the main themes of Matthew 6:19-34 (which we hope you've now memorized), let us remember the profound truth that our earthly possessions and anxieties pale in comparison to the eternal treasures and peace found in God. Jesus calls us to shift our focus from the fleeting and perishable to the everlasting and incorruptible. By investing in heavenly treasures and trusting in God's providence, we align our hearts with his kingdom and his righteousness.

Our daily worries about food, clothing, and the future can easily consume us, but Jesus gently reminds us that our Heavenly Father knows our needs and values us deeply. Just as he provides for the birds of the air and clothes the lilies of the field, he will surely care for us.

Therefore, let us strive to keep our eyes healthy, filled with the light of God's truth and love. In doing so, our whole being will be full of light, reflecting his glory to those around us. We cannot serve both God and money, so let us wholeheartedly choose to serve God, finding freedom from anxiety through faith in his perfect provision (Psalm 34:10).

As we seek first the kingdom of God and his righteousness, we can rest assured that all our needs will be met. Let us cast our anxieties on him, for he cares for us (1 Peter 5:7), and live each day with the confidence that our future is securely held in his hands (Psalm 31:15). Today, let us embrace the peace that comes from trusting in our faithful and loving God, knowing that he is sufficient for all our tomorrows.

Matthew 6:19–34

LAY UP TREASURES IN HEAVEN

19 "Do not lay up for yourselves treasures on earth,
where moth and rust destroy and where thieves break
in and steal, 20 but lay up for yourselves treasures in
heaven, where neither moth nor rust destroys and
where thieves do not break in and steal. 21 For where
your treasure is, there your heart will be also.

22 "The eye is the lamp of the body. So, if your eye is
healthy, your whole body will be full of light, 23 but
if your eye is bad, your whole body will be full of
darkness. If then the light in you is darkness, how
great is the darkness!

24 "No one can serve two masters, for either he will
hate the one and love the other, or he will be devoted
to the one and despise the other. You cannot serve
God and money.

DO NOT BE ANXIOUS

25 "Therefore I tell you, do not be anxious about your life,
what you will eat or what you will drink, nor about your
body, what you will put on. Is not life more than food, and
the body more than clothing? 26 Look at the birds of the
air: they neither sow nor reap nor gather into barns, and
yet your heavenly Father feeds them. Are you not of more
value than they? 27 And which of you by being anxious can
add a single hour to his span of life? 28 And why are you
anxious about clothing? Consider the lilies of the field, how
they grow: they neither toil nor spin, 29 yet I tell you, even
Solomon in all his glory was not arrayed like one of these.
30 But if God so clothes the grass of the field, which today
is alive and tomorrow is thrown into the oven, will he not
much more clothe you, O you of little faith? 31 Therefore do
not be anxious, saying, 'What shall we eat?' or 'What shall
we drink?' or 'What shall we wear?' 32 For the Gentiles seek
after all these things, and your heavenly Father knows that
you need them all. 33 But seek first the kingdom of God and
his righteousness, and all these things will be added to you.

34 "Therefore do not be anxious about tomorrow, for
tomorrow will be anxious for itself. Sufficient for the day is
its own trouble."

Continue the Journey

We hope this devotional has helped you dive deeper into God's Word and that you store many of these verses in your heart to draw from when financial worries press in. This may be the end of the devotional, but we hope you will continue your journey by exploring some of these helpful resources:

Certified Kingdom Advisor (CKA®) // faithfi.com/find
Certified Kingdom Advisor® professionals have met high standards in character, competence, and experience and have been trained to provide biblical financial advice to help you make the most of the resources God has entrusted to you.

FaithFi App // app.faithfi.com
Every day, you can make wise financial decisions with the help of the FaithFi app. This money management tool securely connects to your bank accounts and encourages you to faithfully steward the resources God has entrusted to you. Download FaithFi from the App Store or Google Play Store.

Christian Credit Counselors // christiancreditcounselors.org
If you are struggling with credit card debt, Christian Credit Counselors may be able to help. As an underwriter of FaithFi, Christian Credit Counselors is a trusted resource to help you get out of credit card debt that may be causing you financial anxiety.

For more resources related to this devotional, go to faithfi.com/sparrows

NOTES

NOTES

FAITH FI

FaithFi *equips* Christians with tools and resources to *integrate* faith and financial decisions for the *glory of God*. Our vision is that all Christians would see *God* as their ultimate *treasure*.